LOVE AND THE WAYS WE'VE HEALED

Alaina DaRin

This book is for my lovely partner, Matthew. Thank you so much for loving me unconditionally and being there for me every step of the way. I love this journey with you.
To all of my friends. It has been a wonderful time getting to know you and connecting with you as my soul family.

CONTENTS

1. Eyes of the Heart   1

2. Faith in the Journey   2

3. Celestial   3

4. Honesty   4

5. Awaken   5

6. Healing   6

7. Dreams   7

8. Eternal   8

9. Soul Ablaze   9

10. Sovereign   10

11. Evolving   11

12. Mend   12

13. Caress   13

14. Visions   14

15. Lightbearer   15

16. Enigma   16

17. Liberation   17

18. Elixir   18

19. Remedy   19

20. Vitalize   20

21. Revived   21

22. Burning   22

23. Shelter   23

24. Heaven   24

25. Worthy   25

26. Unraveling   26

27. Chaos   27

28. Coated Skies   28

29. Enchanted   29

30. Illusions   30

31. Incarnate   31

32. Inhibitions   32

33. Letting Go   33

34. Expansion   34

35. Bared   35

36. Every Dimension   36

37. Absolution   37

38. Confessions   38

39. Fallen   39

40. Embrace   40

41. Passionate Souls   41

42. Unconditional   42

43. Self-Love   43

44. Finding Home   44

45. Safety   45

46. Destined   46

47. Fly   47

48. Holy Lovers   48

49. Never-Ending   49

50. Brazen and Free   50

51. Let Me Fall   51

52. Angel Whispers   52

53. Break Open   53

54. Soulful Desire   54

55. Beginnings   55

56. Vulnerable   56

57. Poets in Love   57

58. Transformed   58

59. Heroes   59

60. Crystal Castles   60

61. Trusting the Process   61

About Author   62

Eyes of the Heart

I trusted you
   when I couldn't see myself
   How could your eyes
   be more beautiful?
   How did they see
   more in me?
   Maybe mine are broken,
   but I have you to show me
   what is real

Faith in the Journey

How strong of you to move alone;
   how precious has
   this journey been
   to move with faith
   for a better day?

CELESTIAL

OUR WORLDS HAD COLLIDED,
and you and I
created magic

HONESTY

I DON'T THINK WE need
   to push down our feelings;
   they can come up for air
   if they need to breathe
   If we suffocate every emotion,
   then we're not being honest,
   and we owe it to ourselves
   to hold the space
   for what we feel

Awaken

You showed her body
    how to pray,
    and now her faith
    will never be
    the same

Healing

Our scars were deep,
but our love ran deeper

DREAMS

WALKING INTO THE SHADOWS,
   I was living in a nightmare
   and loving you
   in my dreams

ETERNAL

NOTHING IN THIS LIFE will last,
   so let's hold on to this moment;
   it's all we have

Soul Ablaze

Fire, fire, in my soul,
  burning brightly,
  it's all I know

Sovereign

If we can't live wild,
we can't live free

Evolving

THE PAIN IS NOT a place we stay;
it's where we grow

MEND

MAY WE HEAL
from the wounds
we've been too afraid
to feel

CARESS

HOW DO I BEGIN
   to describe our love
   when it is something
   that can only be
   felt?

VISIONS

I HAD ANOTHER DREAM of you,
   but the best part was
   I didn't even need
   to close my eyes

LIGHTBEARER

THE WORLD CARRIES DARKNESS,
   and yes, so do you
   But you have the chance
   to shine your light
   and remind the world
   what's true

Enigma

She was my nightmare,
   the kind you don't recover from,
   the kind you can't escape

LIBERATION

SHE REALIZED
   it was more important
   to love and to be free
   than to be chained
   by society

ELIXIR

OUR THOUGHTS WERE NOTHING less
    than intoxicating,
    and you were the elixir
    for my saving

Remedy

ANOINT ME WITH YOUR touch
  so that I can feel you
  when I'm hollow

VITALIZE

I'M GRATEFUL THAT
  you tore down my walls
  and showed me
  how beautiful it was
  to break

Revived

We were broken when we met
but we learned to love
with every piece

BURNING

I'LL TELL YOU WHEN to stop,
  but right now
  I need this moment
  Just tell me that
  it'll be alright,
  and we'll make it through
  this fire

SHELTER

EVERY WAVE CAME CRASHING in,
   and every storm released its hail
   I ran for cover
   to the place I knew;
   I found my shelter
   in the depths of you

Heaven

Show me ecstasy
and where your hands will work
because I finally know
what it means to feel,
and it's forever
in your arms

WORTHY

YOU FOUND ME
   paralyzed on the floor,
   no hope
   for a better tomorrow
   But you changed the way I see;
   you changed the way I feel;
   everything in me
   changed for the better

Unraveling

INTRICATE AND BEAUTIFUL,
    we were unfolding
    Our hearts were blessed
    by the heavens
    and our souls were merging

CHAOS

.

THIS WAS OUR CHAOS;
　　this was how stars should break
　　Shattered amongst them,
　　spilling blindly,
　　waiting on wandering hearts
　　to keep

COATED SKIES

YOUR SOUL KNEW MY name,
 and I knew your heart
  We were painting every color
  into the blazing sky

Enchanted

LET'S DANCE IN TIME
   and lose ourselves;
   only our love
   can break the spell

ILLUSIONS

STEPPING OUTSIDE THE KNOWN is scary,
   but how will we seek passion
   if we are confined
   to our mental chains?

INCARNATE

WOULD YOU LOVE ME still
   if I lost my skin?
   Would you love me still
   if I didn't incarnate
   to the time you're in?

INHIBITIONS

TWO SOFTENED HEARTS,
   falling through
   our depth and dark
   What a beautiful coincidence,
   coming together
   without inhibitions

LETTING GO

SOFT AND YIELDING,
   we were flowing with the current
   This was our strength,
   our surrender,
   the power
   in letting go

EXPANSION

WE DIDN'T BELONG ANYWHERE
  We were transcending and exploring
  these thoughts and feelings
  Our hearts were the compass
  and our souls were the map
  and here we have found
  our way back home

Bared

THE GREATEST INTIMACY
was baring
my soul to you
and you loving
every inch

Every Dimension

Visit me in my dreams;
  it's a reality
  that will never change

ABSOLUTION

PARTED LIPS
  bleed a whisper
  Gently begging,
  seeking redemption
  like a quiet sinner

CONFESSIONS

WE HAD TEARFUL CONFESSIONS,
  but nothing out of the ordinary;
  we were painfully ordinary
  Every little thing that excited us
  pulled us towards the edge
  Were we really this imperfect?
  Were we ready for this change?

FALLEN

GIVING HOPE
  Giving tomorrow
  Giving love
  Giving knowledge
  This was our love,
  our pure intentions
  We found our haven,
  a place to stay in,
  because when we fell,
  we also landed

EMBRACE

SOMETHING IN ME HAD changed
 I was tired,
 tired of always asking for something,
 tired of believing a lie
 Instead,
 I started embracing myself
 All of my wants
 All of my desires
 All of my imperfections
 Isn't it beautiful
 when what we want
 and who we are
 align so effortlessly
 that we don't even need to fight;
 we can keep on living our dream?

PASSIONATE SOULS

THERE'S NOTHING WRONG WITH desire
   We suffer soulfully,
   all the time
   We can't hold on too tightly,
   but we can hold on to
   what makes us happy
   In the end,
   we know our souls seek passion
   because they look for it
   in every lifetime

Unconditional

You've always been so honest,
  and I appreciate that so much
  I've always known
  that I could be myself
  because you were never one to judge

SELF-LOVE

SOME SAY THAT TO love another,
   you must first love yourself
   But I've loved another
   with all my heart,
   and I was still learning how
   to love myself

Finding Home

Awakening to your truth
  feels like abundance to the soul,
  freedom to travel
  through time and space
  Awakening to your truth
  feels like finding Home,
  to find true love
  in any place

SAFETY

YOU HOLD ME IN your arms,
   and you make me feel so safe
   You protect me from these shadows
   and revive me of my faith
   When I look into your eyes,
   all my doubts
   slip away

DESTINED

THERE WAS SOMETHING BEAUTIFUL,
  special,
  about the way we were
  It didn't matter
  the time or space
  we existed in
  because we would always find
  each other

FLY

IF WE ARE HONEST with ourselves,
   no matter what it is about,
   we will start feeling pieces of ourselves
   breaking off
   and turning into birds

Holy Lovers

TENDERNESS IS YOUR NAME;
   our hearts collide as one
   We have come here many lifetimes
   just to feel our love
   Many forms to our existence,
   our purpose written in the stars
   We collide like holy lovers;
   our love has healed these scars

NEVER-ENDING

ENCHANTED BY YOUR BRILLIANCE
  Lending me your light,
  guiding me home,
  you were the one
  The angels had told me
  this was our story
  Our dreams unveiled the mystery;
  that our love is
  never-ending

Brazen and Free

You filled me up
   to the hilt,
   where tears could flow
   brazen and free
   You granted me
   my only wish,
   to have the courage
   to just be me

LET ME FALL

SOFTNESS IN YOUR EYES,
   our love sent me wild
   Promise you won't stop me,
   promise you won't catch me,
   just let me fall
   into our destiny

ANGEL WHISPERS

SPEAK TO ME IN stars,
   like floating angels
   dancing around my head

Break Open

Our hearts will break,
  just as they should
  For how can we hold
  a love so strong
  if we don't break open?

Soulful Desire

We were hungry for something
only our souls could taste

Beginnings

AFTER ALL THE POURING rain,
  we finally stopped asking for the sun
  We saved every drop because
  our hearts were thirsty for love
  Once we tasted the cleansing,
  our hunger was now for change
  We embraced these new beginnings
  because our lives would never be the same

Vulnerable

You made me feel vulnerable,
   and I didn't know
   if that was okay
   But I let go,
   piece by piece,
   and finally,
   it was okay

POETS IN LOVE

YOUR WORDS,
    they flow at random
    Your words tell stories,
    and your eyes
    tell secrets;
    I am infatuated
    with your soul

Transformed

YOU ARE LOVED
   more than you know
   Can you feel it;
   moving inside you,
   changing you?

HEROES

WE WAIT FOR HEROES
hoping we will be saved,
but maybe
it was always us
who was worth the wait

CRYSTAL CASTLES

WE WERE LEARNING,
   healing,
   living in crystal castles
   Speaking softly,
   moving gently,
   lest they easily break
   All the while,
   we were burning,
   fueled by purpose and passion
   That was our strength,
   our surrender,
   the delicate process
   of our crystallization

TRUSTING THE PROCESS

I WANTED TO BE messy;
 to rid myself of my perfectionistic ways
 Was I succeeding?
 Was I letting go?
 Perhaps we'll find ourselves in happenstance,
 perhaps we'll trust the flow

ABOUT AUTHOR

Alaina is a writer and poet living in Central New York with her fiancé, Matthew. When she isn't working or writing, she enjoys walks in nature, late-night drives, drinking coffee, and listening to music.

71252102R00040